AUTUMN

By

JON BICKLEY

First published 2020
ISBN: 9781661848248

About The Author.

Jon Bickley was born in London on 23rd October 1956. He is a poet, a folksinger and a songwriter. As a child he heard hymns in church, his mother singing Palgrave's Golden Treasury and the Beatles. Later it was Kerouac, Shakespeare and the Marx Brothers, now it is Yeats, Burnside and Heaney. Nothing much changes. He has self-published 3 volumes of poetry, released a dozen albums and is host of the Invisible Folk Club radio show and podcast. Jon has contributed to the collaborative writing project known as For The Many Not The Few in volumes 2- 12. Find out more about Jon on the link - www.jonbickley.com

Contents –

How Do You Live In Autumn?

I.

We met in Summer
and I was running bewildered
at the loss of Spring's blossom
I thought it would always be there.
The doe in the field
ran from mate to mate
filling the field with babies
as the leaves filled the trees
and your buds were open
splayed to the sun

I was drawn to your heat
but I couldn't understand your wrath
I flew around you
but the flame despises the moth

I reached out a hand
I don't know if you noticed.

2.

A wolf was caught in a trap
and was sleeping on a rock
on a ledge high up in the mountains.
An eagle hovered above her
and glided down,
singing "Come, fly with me
what things I can show you,
what things we will see."

The wolf hid her bloody ankle
under her body
so no one could see,
not even her.
She said "I am just sleeping.
It is normal to sleep.
We do it every day.
It is pleasant to sleep.
I will just stay here
and sleep."

3.

But how do you live in Autumn?
There are enough green leaves on the trees
that you can make believe that summer is still here,
but most of them have gone
and it rains for a long long time
and I sit by my window and wonder where it all went,
those sunny meadows,
those drooping boughs
heavy with fertility.

How do you live in Autumn
if all you have to talk about
is what Summer was like?
The trees are balding;
dripping leaves and rain,
the path is slippery
with mud and leaves
but there is fire
and gods
and time to write
and dream.

In my imagination
it is time for me to land,
time for me to stake out
a patch of land
and call it mine.

I don't know how I lost my grip
maybe I was holding something else
and it is no longer Summer
and is now Autumn.
I have to put my feet on this ground
to sit by this fire,
at this desk,
under this hill
with these birds.

How do you live in Autumn
when everything around you is dying?
Put people in the picture.
People in boots and hats,
coats and scarves.
People puffing up the hill,
people with a fire to gather around.

How do you live in Autumn
when everything around you is dying
and you cannot rely on what you
see on the next tree
as being dead or alive?
You have to build your own fire.

The Rain Sits In The Air

The rain sits in the air defying gravity,
it is neither day or night.
Time takes a rest on a bench
at the top of a hill,
"This is what living in clouds
must be like" he says.

The hill is home to birds' eggs
and dead branches,
to leaf fall and green shoot,
the circus comes and goes
and for each season
there is someone spellbound
and wondered for the first time,
every change is new to someone.

But I have sat here with my pen in my hand
for time beyond remembering.
I have seen the moon's guests arrive
until the party is so full
it spills out into our minds
and makes us sing
the victory over darkness
that makes us invisible to ourselves.
I have seen the rain hang in the air
as it wants to talk to us.

The Frost Clings To The Leaves.

The frost clings to the leaves
and the mist curls up alongside
the hedgerow
nuzzling the trees
white grass blankets
the meadow
in the bed of nature
it is early morning
and the world is still asleep.

The cold has coated the field
like the marble of a Roman statue
with the grip of an ancient fossil;
a memory of what once was
so cold it is forgotten and gone
it is as if summer never existed.

We are entering the slumber of Winter
the cold has held our bones
and we can see only death and decay,
colder and colder mornings
until the coldness becomes all there is
and we do not wake.

And yet we know that change continues
and after the impossible
comes the possible again.

Leaf.

She woke one day to find it was Autumn.
The leaves on the tree outside her window
were brown and yellow,
the life drained out of them
sometime ago,
but they were still there
clinging like a memory of the Summer.

She lay down to sleep
and a north wind blew.
In the morning the leaves were gone
and the branch,
released from its weight
sprang up
and dreamed of Spring.

Birthday Card.

If you roll up the carpet of the world
Argentinians wake up on Bondi Beach
New Yorkers wake up on the Great Wall of China
And I wake up in Moscow.

The International Date Line
lays down with the Greenwich Meridian
and we all wake up yesterday.

If I roll up this birthday card of yours
you are still holding your children's hands
on their first day at school,
still waiting up for them on their first date,
still picking their toys up from the floor.

On the occasion of your birthday
I want to give you a present.
I want to give you your now
I want to give you the moment
you moved out of the family home
and claimed your life as your own.
I want to give you your Independence Day.
Walk out. Walk out now. Don't look back
and unroll the world and see it at your feet.

A Sonnet For Today (08.03.2016).

When the bomb went off I was blown across the room
and the darkness was upon me like they closed up the
tomb,
and each bomb is marked with an individual's name
and no two bombs are ever the same
and the one that landed on you threw nails into the air;
shrapnel for the face, napalm for the hair
limbs were shattered and tears were shed
for the loss of innocence, for the maimed and the dead
and nothing will ever be the same again.
But I will search for a hand in the rubble
and I will remove each stone and lift each head
and I will hold your broken body until I feel you breathe
again
and then together we will build a new home from the old
and so the hill of survival will be built from the rubble of
despair.

Call It Love.

She is awash with sunlight.
She has walked in it to get here
splashing at her feet
falling from the sky
dripping from her hair
into her eyes
and from her clothes

It has bounced off her sunglasses
and her watch and her camera
She is wet with it;
it has soaked into her
and pulses around her like a halo
beating in her blood
swelling her heart
loosening her thighs and belly
throbbing in her vagina
and her eyes shine.

His skin is red because he has been close to her
He has stood where others have fled
He has been in the presence of that fire
Been in the presence of that sun
Call it love.

Love Is Not Comfortable.

Love is not comfortable
Love is not easy
Love does not make you happy

Love is a meteor
that travels across galaxies
in order to hit you
and only you

It hits your head
It burns a hole in your brain
and sits in your chest
burning every organ
until smoke comes out of your mouth
and you cannot see what is in front of you

Love is not an anniversary
or a candle lit dinner
or sex or a gift.
Love is the threshing floor.

Where You Separate Wheat From Chaff.

Love is a pool in the desert
and you know how easy it is to drown in the desert.
We are so desperate
We run towards it
We dive in
And we don't come out.

If you want a happy life
avoid love at all costs.
If you want to feel alive
chase love whatever the cost.

Christmas Lights.

When I look up at the Christmas lights
I think about that star
and wonder how it looks to you
wherever you are

Since the mine closed down
the town just washed away
The young men hang around in the street
and the old men never go out

The library has gone
and been replaced by a bookmakers
and what happened to my cow
and a couple of acres?

Does anyone know
where the broad road will lead?
Spending money we don't have
own things we don't need

Whoever you were
Whoever you are
Get out on the road
and follow that star.

Merry Christmas Everyone.

Merry Christmas everyone
tis the season of goodwill
when you eat and drink
enough to make a donkey ill
when you buy each other presents
that no one can afford
and watch so much television
that everyone ends up getting bored
and the kids nudge Grandma
to check she's still alive
and the husband is having another drink
waiting for her mother to arrive
and the wife is looking beautiful
wearing long sleeves
dreading the time
when the guests all leave
and under the tree
a month's salary is spent
but the job is finished
since that European contract went
darling, I didn't get you what you asked for
I got you this instead
and she tries not to look disappointed
and wonders when she can go off to bed
and each present
has fifteen minutes of fame
and every bloody Christmas

is always the same
and somewhere outside
Mary and Joseph are looking for a home.

They Came Up A Mountain.

I met a man travelling from Nazareth to Bethlehem
he wanted to show me his ID card and letters of transit
he said he'd been through 100 checkpoints
his pregnant wife was hiding under a blanket

I said I'm a stranger here myself
but that many people were leaving the city up ahead
where fire rained down out of the sky
they said it turned the sea black and the sky red

He said that he's been travelling all day and all night
his wife and his donkey needed to get some sleep
but the clouds were closing in on him
and his mountain path was steep.

They came up the mountain to get away from the flood
and now there's a crack in the mountain.

At This Time Of Year.

At this time of year
it is tempting to surrender
to the shadows
the short dark days
the melancholy rain

It is easier to think
of all the things you have done wrong
to think of the things you love
that have been taken away from you,
the endless winter of it all

But I am here to remind you
that there was joy
there was laughter and music
and sun and love

There were kind words
when you couldn't speak them,
poems when you couldn't hear them,
songs when you couldn't sing them,

And there can be again
come, take my hand,
step into the light.

I Stepped Through An Archway Of Stars.

I stepped through an archway of stars
Into a desert at night
and sat beneath a tree
to strum on my guitar

I know you have sat beneath a tree
and watched the apples fall
and like Eve gorged yourself
on as many as you can
and in the morning suffered such heart burn.

The night settles on me
like the hood of my cloak
and music rests on me
like a blessing
like the laying on of hands
like the black leaves
pealing from the night sky
and the space from which they come
lets in the music of the spheres
throbbing and glowing
in the desert night.

And the spirit is upon me
And the darkness trails about me
Cascading starlight and wonder

When the spirit is upon me it is not me who speaks
but those black leaves that speak through me,
given utterance by my stillness.
Beneath this tree in the desert,
by the night falling,
by the gentle strumming of my guitar.
Listen, can you hear it?
Can you hear it above your breathing?
Can you feel the black leaves falling?
Can you hear the music coming through the holes in the
night sky?
Such sounds. Such light. Such night.
This world is suspended in night and the music takes
over.
Can you hear it?
Can you feel my hand in yours?
Can you hear the words of the poet?

Tom's House.

I am sitting in a courtyard,
the household is still asleep
and the sun touches my face
in the attendant way
my old lover would
from time to time.

A few yellow leaves drop to the table,
early September in the north of England
flowers in pots are still waking up
some look to the sun
some look a little hung over.

Music has filled my week
accordion, guitar and songs,
sitting by day and remembering
the shape of the song's body,
where it moves and where it gives
the step it finds easy
and the place where it stumbles.
And then in the evening, the friends
the bars, the songs, camaraderie
and then home for rum and bed,
this week has reawakened a joy
that has been long dormant

I know I have to go back to the South

and make peace with the taxman
but for now I have this moment
with the sun's fingers on my face.

.

There Was A Knock At The Door.

There was a knock at the door,
the singers continued singing
and I rose, eager to greet my guest
for I knew who was knocking.
Faithful to the minute of her arrival.
I opened the door and the black
pavilion of her hair was lit up
by the red sun of her lips.
The hills of Lebanon rose from her blouse
and her nails were swordfishes
leaping from the Indian Ocean,
her body was a bell and her soul rang out.

She entered her home from home and found welcome.

I returned to the singers
and before she had sat down
I had picked up my guitar
and conjured a memory
a deep heart
a song that reached into her gut
and grabbed her spine
she stood transfixed
my voice shook
"Your touch took root in my heart,"
a root that still exists in both of us
traced deep underground

knowing that it would surface
in a new place
and put forth new shoots, new blossoms.

The Fat Poet.

The fat poet perched upon his chair
and tucked his legs under the desk
so his short arms would reach the page.

The fire crackled behind him
and before him, the impenetrable night
as implacable as a blank page

He rocked a little in his chair
and the aroma of words rose within him
strong and dark

And when she read his words
it was as if she rolled his body
in her hand like a brandy glass

The words were fire in her mouth
lava in her lungs
and life in her belly

She stirred a ferment
the smell, the taste, the heat
of his meaning intoxicating her

And as he stared out at the wintery sky
he picked out the moon and the stars
to lay at her feet.

A Tree.

There is a space in the forest
where your tree should be
and as a result
the trees around you
are growing out of shape.
They are spreading
and bending
into the space that you
should be occupying.

You are not being kind
giving them more space
to grow
You are actually causing them
to grow up wrong
causing them to be
bent out of shape
because you are not occupying
your space in the forest

And one day
that will result in resentment, anger
and disappointment.

Can you feel it?

The answer is simple.

Find your place in the forest
and grow to your full height.

Poetry Is Sex For The Soul.

The sun is rising and there's no one else around
roll over and stretch
see the light in the trees
outside your window
I am with you always
I am beside you

The sunlight on the leaves
drives away all fear
Your body makes everything clear
as I whisper the secrets of the universe in your ear

These words are where all things start
This voice will make you whole
Music is healing for the heart
and poetry is sex for the soul

Stars dance in my hand
and the moon rises in my eye
I kiss your hip
I kiss your thigh
I extol the beauty of your body
I extol the wisdom of your mind

I extol your very soul
The guards have gone
There's no patrol

You are alone
with your soul

And with these words
I will sit in your soul
in the morning we will stroll

In the Garden of Eden
freed, when the world was new
Naked spirits set free
Songbirds singing in the trees.

The Heart.

The heart is subject to a thousand foes
a thousand woes
and a thousand blows.
It is whipped
and dipped in dirt
and taken out and hurt

Every day you take your life in your hands
offer it up, and hope for something more than yesterday.

Then you drop your arms and march on.

Some of us deny it.
Some of us defy it.
But you cannot lie about it,
it's hard on the heart.

But when Aretha sang
she healed the heart,
every time.

Black.

At no stage did she ever fully
emerge from the shadows,
even in direct sunlight
there was always a shade
in the back of her mind
a distraction in her eye
a pallor in her cheek.

Her wardrobe overflowed
with characters she had
recruited from car boot sales
and cast into her plays.
Purple lace and whalebone
polka dots and feather boas
bursting over her bed
like a tsunami of daydreams
but when it came to getting dressed
she usually went back to black

She pulls on her boots as Autumn comes
and pulls that black coat
from the back of her wardrobe
some girls just look good in black.

Brexit.

In hindsight the last couple of years were pretty bad;
They were arguing all the time.
She went ahead and bought those curtains without asking
him.
He played football all weekend.
I wonder if it because she wanted to go to Lesbos and I
didn't.

Anyway, now he's on a mate's sofa
and doesn't know what to do with himself.
His mates bring pizza and cheap lager round
and play games.
At the end of the evening there's that awkward moment
when theirs meet
and they can't think of what to say.
A quick slap on the arm
and out of the door.
He goes back to the couch but cannot sleep
without her breathing, her warmth,
the way he'd listen to hear if she would talk in her sleep
in case she said another man's name.

She has friends round all the time.
Morning coffee, lunch, wine in the evening.
Gross generalisations about gross men,
better off without him,
now you can get on with your life.

When he does talk, he talks about nothing else.
He used to be quite good on football and movies
now, all there is, is what she said about this
what she said about that
as if he is trying to convince himself
that it was her decision.
But it wasn't.
It was his.
His decision to shoot himself in the foot
Most guys secretly wish they were in a relationship as
good as that.
And when they are not,
They don't know what to do with themselves.

I suppose he'll have to go and get his stuff soon.
I hope he doesn't bring it here.

The Sunday.

From a train window heading south
the glory of the morning took my breath away
flashing sunlight burst upon my eye
shouting the opening up of the new day

The sunlight fell like butterflies
flickering celestial guests
like the bright hypnotic fleeting
lightness of your breasts

The flashing brightness of the sun
set in a rippling ocean of blue
drowning and transporting
when her blue eyes look at you

and the choir in Heaven
singing the sun up to the sky
is the new light in your hair
and the exultation on high

Your eyes are two dancing planets
spinning in the blue
and your hair is a song sung by your soul
the sunrise of you.

"But we are old, in the evening of our lives
shadows are filling the orbits of my eyes.

I hear what you say about beauty but how can it be?
Do you mock me with your poetry?"

The sun is new every morning
and looks like it did the day before
but has been around forever
the oldest thing you ever saw

Like the sun we age
as every solstice goes by
but like the sun you are beautiful
dappled and blinking in my eye

So be like the sun and rise up
let your blessing fall on all you survey
glow for me baby
there's beauty in those rays.

I Went Walking In The Garden Of Love.

Pt I.

I went walking in the garden of love,
branches like witches fingers
and a lonely magpie above
while January lingers

I went to the pool where the oracle spoke
but the pool was frozen hard
no light, no warmth,
no muse for the bard

No song, no poem, no spring shoot
No crack in the ice
under the persuasion of my boot.

This hasty green shoot
is impatient to aspire
to flower.
Impatient to see his own reflection
in the limpid pool.

I Went Walking In The Garden Of Love.

Pt 2.

The husks of last year's fruit
crop up unexpectedly
and cause me to stumble
while there is no sign
of what is to come
no buds, no birds in flight
no divination in the Heavens
just clouds, still, grey clouds.
I sigh and my breath
forms a plume of white vapour
which disappears
before the Spirit can hover
or useful metaphor appears.

Birthday.

Birthdays count time from the crying moment
we pushed through the fleshy curtains into this room
but all of us catch echoes of a time before that
a time that we cannot focus on
So strong were the hospital lights
So loud the family greeting
So faint the echo, so fleeting the moment.

In order to pin it we imagine it was a world like this
and we were a deer, a crocodile, and a weaver
but we could just have easily been dust on the rings of
Saturn.
And there are echoes radiating forward from birth
moments of recognition
of "Yes"
of easing the shoulders
and coming home
Moments, passing moments

A bird settles and flies on
but in these moments
we become aware of that other life .....
that eternal life

This is our inheritance –
not the overcrowded commute

From birth to death
Not the bruises of childhood
or the inadvertent cruelty of parents

but the echoes of stories
pictures of moments
a place to pause
increasingly a place to live
Happy Birthday my dear, you are looking well
You are as old as the stories you tell.

Dance Hall.

I left the dance hall a while back
and came to sit in the bar
I can still hear the noise through the walls
from this high stool I can
watch people come and go
in the big mirror behind the bar
We started dancing
but drifted apart
as one song slipped into another
I looked at the door to the dance hall
in the mirror
half expecting you
to come and find me
Your Niagara hair
Your flashing blue eyes
Your hands smoothing
out your black dress
Your black hair
Your swirls of mascara
and then my glass is empty
And I look at my reflection in the mirror
and I decide to stay where I am for a bit longer.
If I ever go back in there
it would be to find you
and to dance again
to brush my hand against yours
my hip to your hip

my lips to your lips
but my legs are heavy
my shoes are tight
and I wonder if my dancing days are behind me.

I Will Wait.

A thin film of mist
separates a tree from its reflection
on the lake in the early morning light
above the mist, head tipped back,
exultant in the morning,
below, cloaked and quiet
You know it is there
but you cannot hold it.

What is it that lies beneath your surface?
What reflections are there on your lake?
I know it is there because I have seen
your eyes disappear under water
withdraw and dart away
like fish looking for the reeds
making do with the mist

I will sleep under the tree until the morning
and I will meet you in the silence
in the early morning mist
between the tree and the reflection
between the living and the dead
between the world and the other

As you bow your head
beneath the water
I will wait on the bank

with a pen and a guitar
waiting for you to emerge from your reflection,
exultant in the morning.

Coastline.

Year on year
tide on tide
the lapping waves
the heaving currents
have brought shells and bones
sand and shipwrecks
bodies and ghosts
to make this coastline.

Tall cliffs
a high imposing body
rising out of the sea
bone on bone
turf on turf
tree on tree
a home to bird and beast
a prone and panting land.

Slices fall together
to make a loaf
year on year
birthdays spinning
year on year
sediment laid down
tall cliffs rising
year on year.

Today she moves
with an elegant slowness
her gaze goes ahead of her
like her familiar
sniffing the air
sensing the wind
ears pricked
knowing.

On the cliff the spirit man stands
he feels the wind on his skin
the heat of the sun on his head
his eyes touch the horizon
where the ocean overflows
and his eyes water
in response
he breathes

As I grow older
my body lays down
a cliff, a meadow
a forest for birds to sing
my spirit rises
and stands on the cliff
warm in the eternal sun
ready to join hands
and sing.

Mother.

When I was a baby
I breathed in your fear
like a swarm of bees.

You didn't have a mother
so you didn't know what to do
and they buzzed around you
all the time.

Often one would escape
and sting someone
with a spiteful comment.

I didn't know if that was
a desire to hurt
or a defensive force field
of static electricity,
and electrified fence
that would crackle and spark
morning, noon and night,
never earthed
never discharged
rogue lightning.

When the bees were asleep
I was the rising sun
in a world of stars,

but it didn't take much
to wake them. Just someone
failing to notice that I was the sun.

They stung my heart with jealousy
they stung my mind with doubt,
and they stung my feet with fear.

I would leave the party before I had arrived.
I would doubt the girl before I had loved.

And later I would quell the bees
with a drink and a smoke
with boredom and absence.

But now the queen is old
and senses her own death
and the swarm is preparing to leave.

Tree Sonnet.

When I was bringing up my three children
we lived near the woods and I took them there
to walk amongst the trees and feel the peace.
Those trees were my cathedral and my church.
Time is different there; it's longer, slower,
their roots touch the soil as I never will
their leaves touch Heaven as I never will
Superior beings singing God's song
This is a way of living together.
On a good day you can feel them talking
on a good day they will bless your walking
roots like legs, skin like bark, leaves on the ground
if you listen you can hear the quiet,
at one with the land, one with the weather.

The Poet Has A Hundred Tales To Tell.

I cannot read what I did not write
for all the noise I've heard
Moving into battle with the air
Inspiration must be spurred

Give me a tune, give me a voice
give me a righteous word
Give me the courage to sing my song
give me ears to be heard

As the sun sinks behind the hill
and the shadows touch the sky
and the trees come to dreaming life
right before your eyes

And the stars flicker in the darkness
and the flames flicker in the grate
I'll tell you a story
before it gets too late

Flocks of birds will bring messages
trees clap their hands and sing
the flags are raised and flags torn down
flags are a foolish thing

And the poet pushes his boat into the sea
with the stars as his chart

and drags his story in the waves,
in the tides of your heart

Let the muse fall upon me
I will fall under her spell
Gather round my friends
the poet has a hundred tales to tell.

Productivity Bonus.

The productivity bonus will make all the difference this
year
now the wife's not earning and the rent is in arrears
the food bank gave us what little Christmas we enjoy
now the kids and half the street are unemployed

We make a bit of a wing for a fighter jet
it's about as international as you can get
a bit in France, a bit in Spain
I just go to work, and then I go home again.

And the Minister for Defence lays a wreath in November
and then leads a trade delegation he will always remember
a cocktail reception with ice and lemon
and a contract to kill children in Syria and Yemen

Thank God you still have your job, Dad
hate to think where we'd be
at least we've got a roof over our head
and decorations and presents and turkey.

When I Don't Write I Get Sick.

When I don't write I get sick
Jagged little letters lodge in my muscles
Punctuation stops my arteries
I ache and I sneeze incoherent syllables.

Numb to my emotions
forgetful of the argument
this way or that
no tide in the blood
no gravity in the moonlight
no shadow in the night

In the gym young men lift weights
break sweat, build and sculpt their bodies
It takes a different kind of strength to lift this pen
and build a body of work.

Silence should come with a health warning.

We Stood In The Night.

We stood in the night
under January stars
so white that no eye
could stand more
than a few pin pricks
in the blanket sky

Our breath hymned
the night with its own
white mist
bride's maid to the moon
beneath a congregation of stars.

You wrapped me around
your finger
and I placed a star there
our eyes streaming
at its brilliance.

Open The Book.

Open the book
smooth the page
pick up the pen
and wait.

A boy on a bike in a field
a runner looking at his watch
cars hiss by in the rain
the rain and the rain
the broken gutter sends a river down my wall
one day it will wear a canyon
into my house
and the rain will cease to be my neighbour
and become my wife.

Tabla and gamelan
at my window.

Droplets picked up in the Indian Ocean
Refugeed across Africa
Dumped in the Atlantic
left to drown
until the beneficent Gulf Stream
swept it up
tossed in the air like a bowler
and pitched at my white framed wicket.
Rain is our common wealth

despite the voice of Cnut in the street
we need the rain
our gardens, our fields, our streets,
my gutter needs the rain
to sing me its song.

Rain Clouds In June.

Rain clouds in June
Magpie is sitting in the tree
calling for his mate
but all he gets is rain clouds in June
Magpie sitting in a tree
shouting at the sky
but all he gets is rain clouds in June
Magpie sitting in a tree
singing one for sorrow
and he gets rain clouds in June
Magpie sitting in a tree
calling for rain
and here comes the rain in June
I called you up to meet you
and this time you picked up
I remember our shared table
The knife and the loving cup
The spooning and the candle
The sitting down, the getting up
but that was all so long ago
and we didn't see it right
and my feasting companion
ran out into the night
I waited until morning
I waited until she came back
and when she did the banquet resumed
and all the guests were served

wine and flesh were consumed
we gorged until morning
we drank the whole night through
and sometimes a guest left
and was replaced by someone new
and sometimes we ate the food
and sometimes we ate the guests
sometimes the feast was damned
and sometimes it was blessed
and now I am going to see you
after all these years
there is still loyalty, sympathy
help and support.
A beauty still lingers there
like a bird in a tree
like one for sorrow
like a rain cloud in June.

Romeo And Juliet Were Weightless.

Romeo and Juliet were weightless
Astronauts in space, walking on no air,
out of their element, buoyed on their love
they bobbed like a bottle on the
ocean, newly unstopped and messageless,
delirious and let loose on love.
I know, they said, let's go for a spacewalk.
Drifting on the creamy stars with Juliet,
he turned over in the bed of the sky.
Gazing at the silver god Romeo,
pulling on the airline that leads to him
pulling him closer and breathing him in,
she slipped from his grasp and floated away.
With one small step, he followed after her.

Polly Higgins Died Today.

Polly Higgins died today aged fifty.
She was a barrister who tried to make it an offence
to damage the environment.
She called it Ecocide and I'm on her side.
In an age when people think barristers make coffee
and everyone has the right to do
what they like and to be offended
by what they do not like, without consequences
When corporations are accountable to no one
not even shareholders
Polly understood the power of the law
the power of words to bring something new into being.
She said that it is a crime to harm the world
and that if the law said so, then criminals would go to jail,
directors made accountable for their decisions,
joint and severely responsible.
It is an offence to all of us
that the world is being
eaten out from under us
that people can hide behind
corporate logos and
do harm to all of us.
What was done in the dark
will be brought into the light.
Polly Higgins died today aged fifty.
She had a good idea, don't let it die.

I Thought I Heard Them Sing.

I thought I heard them sing
or hum, or something like that
the hedgerows are thick in May

Blackthorn clustered together
reaching out sideways to gather the sun
or dance or sing or something like that

There are trees on the top of the hill
it might have been them
gently humming to one another
they say that their roots have
tendrils that link up a whole forest
a choir of trees, a cathedral of leaves
what if the birds just echoed the tree song?

What if they were not the great choir masters
but they were just singing the songs
that the trees taught them?
I will go and sing now
a lonely call hoping for a mighty echo.

Autumn Pt I.

Night came to the door unexpectedly
He introduced his wife as Autumn
and as he entered the room and sat down
His cloak enveloped all of us.

We lit a fire in the Temple of the Night
and lit candles to the sky in lieu of stars;
A spell against the absence of moonlight,
A woman's body mapped out on the wall

Night wrapped his cloak about us
and Autumn glowed in the dark.

Autumn Pt 2.

A soldier on a horse
My grandfather on Snooker
during the First World War
on farmland in summer.

Summer is gone now
and so is he
His picture flickers in candlelight
coming and going

I knew him you know
a man of infinite jest
but fallen now,
like the night.

We light candles to keep our memories alive
and read patterns in the shadows
until we have tidied the past
onto the mantelpiece of tonight

Maybe as the night falls in our minds
we'll remember him more clearly
as my mother does
childhood memories from seventy years ago
dance before her in the room
while she repeats the story she told seven
minutes ago her father has become

A candle passed from hand to hand as her face
flickers in her darkness
And my face flickers in mine.

Autumn Pt 3.

Break out the night
break out the fire
break out pagan spells and magic
release Dionysus from his grave
The flowers of the meadow have faded
and soon night will call forth
the spirit of fire and wine
the full gourd of harvest
The tripping infant
is now the stomping soldier
laying down his weapon
for food and wine
and meditation on the night
for staring at the flames
and seeing your dreams
for turning over in the ocean of the night
and being misled by shadows
phantoms and voices
appear and disappear
in the séance of the darkness
in the ritual of the candles
in the life of fire.

A Summer Sonnet.

The light from the back door
sits on the path like a bird's wing
before it gives way to darkness
and feathers dare not go
You can pick out the shadows
where the shrubs are and
the spreading Liquid Amber
with its promise of return
But now it is summer-and she is gone
my eyes swing up to the sky
like a fairground boat swinging
out of earthly lights into that other realm
where a poet's kisses stud the sky
in the hope that his beloved might look up.

Murmur.

A murmur, the young doctor said
we had better get that checked out.
My heart is murmuring to me
I wonder what it is saying
my doctor thinks it is getting old and tired
that it is not pumping the blood
with the youthful vigour
that once sent a shout into the world.
Now it is just a murmur.
That explains a lot.
Is that like a murmuration of starlings?
Is my heat legion, rippling and
turning inside out in its multitude?
Disparate and connected.
There have been times when I have
not known what to do with myself
so maybe that's it. I am a flock of birds.
Maybe it is the abandoned lover
groaning in the place
where time does not exist
and it is always night.
Love unmet.
A longed for conversation,
A murmur unanswered
A sonar with no echo.
A sob.
Or maybe it is the ceaseless babble

Of poetry. Maybe we all murmur
Maybe the wind and the rain and
the birdsong find an echo in the cave
of the human heart and if you listen closely
enough you can hear what
The human heart is saying.
The articulation of the soul
The speech of the heart
I must attend the murmur in my heart
Listen closely
Obediently scribe
Pass it on

I Am With My Son.

I am with my son
in a coastal town
and the seagulls are taking over
I feel like there is so much to say
as one day steals the next day
and suddenly we are both older
I was telling him about the Roman army
how they left nothing behind
scorched earth and desolation
allegiance to the flag
to the eagle
to the Emperor
To Rome
But the sun is going down
in this sleepy coastal town
and it is getting time to go home
On the drive home
I wonder what sort of life he'll have
when he is driving his son home
Will he keep it the same
or will he change?

Windows.

I.

The walled garden runs down to the unseen road
where the cars sound like waves washing up on the shore

All is dripping with morning
twittering and cackling birdsong
summoning the sunrise
to banish the mist
and start the day
life is too good to waste they say
but the world is not ready to wake
and turns over in its valley
for another hour of sleep.

2.

The mist hangs in the valley
and drips paint down the page
green smears into grey
black for the flagstones
red for the berries
brown for bare branches
yellow leaves at my window
my heart is part of everything I am seeing
as the morning comes dripping into being.

3.

The valley has been taken by a mist
and I cannot see where I must go.
The world was in darkness
an hour ago
now it is grey
the wet fur of a sleeping animal
breathing heavily
dreaming the day into being.

Ancient trees slumber
and sentinel hedges hide the path
to the gate
the household is still asleep

A pale light of an unseen sunrise
reflects on the flagstones
I cannot see where I must go
but each step makes the next clearer.

Earth Sonnets.

I.

The soul of the earth reaches up through the tree
and touches the sky
the soul of the child stirs in its heart
and flies from the eye
and we mingle and stir one with another
one with the world
we shimmer and eddy and dance
as tributaries merge, surging to the ocean.

And yet as one hand is raised to the stars
the other strikes down the temple of trees
lays waste the forest and the fields
send fellow creatures off the edge of existence
we can tell ourselves it is black when it is white
and choose to see day when it is night.

2.

I took my love to the babbling brook
to sit and find harmony with nature
beauty did surround us, we could but look,
she sips water she says is good for her
she is natural and pure and lovely
like the trees and the bees and the birds
she rests her back against an ancient tree
and we kiss for what seems like forever

I wonder which way is back to the car
and why we had to travel so far
my love says there are no trees where we live
despite all the donations that we give
my love drinks her water in natures dream
and drops her bottle in the babbling stream.

Yeoman.

Yeoman can you tell me
why are the birds leaving the trees?
Can you tell me why the lightning strikes the sea?
Can you tell me what is happening to me?

Are we driving out the Romans?
Are we digging up the straight roads?
Are we pulling down the statues?
Is it raining frogs and toads?

Are we clearing out the market?
Driving stakes at the border?
Restoring law and order
for richer or for poorer?

There is a wind blowing in the trees
but the trees do not bend
there is a tear in the curtain
that will not mend

Pirates in suits hiding behind the door
gangsters and cutthroats looking to score
if we destroy what we've got we'll end up with more?
and I don't know what any of this is for

There's a man at a desk in the temple
he'll buy anything you bring,

he'll tell you what it's worth
he'll turn the whole town into money

And I'm standing at the window
waiting for someone to stop us
going round and round in circles
getting poorer all the time

I see fruit rotting on the tree
Vegetables rotting in the field
while farmers argue at the gate
which way an apple is peeled

I saw a cart bogged down in a field
I saw a mother with a heart that could not be healed.
There's a price on your house, a price on your bed
a price on your boots and a price upon your head.

Self-Portrait;

I. Invisible.

When a man is in his sixties he becomes invisible
not to others
Others can see that he's been around a long time
and might know a thing or two
and he might even surprise them
with a bit of wisdom
Others can see he doesn't need to bounce around the
room
because he's just encountered the latest idea.
He has heard it before in a different time
on a different tongue, with a different hair style
but heard it all the same
and he has heard how it didn't work
and got trampled by the next new idea.
Others can see that he can enjoy the respect of the young
but does not curl up and die
when that respect turns to scorn or neglect.
When a man is in his sixties he becomes invisible
to himself.

All my life I have been surprised and delighted
when I have discovered that this body can do this
Ooh look, I can please a woman, play guitar, cradle a
baby.
All my life I have been surprised and delighted

when I have discovered that this brain can do this
Ooh look, I can understand science and history,
bring people together and find common ground.
All my life I have been surprised and delighted
when I have discovered that this heart can do this
Ooh look, I can reach into the dark and touch a soul
encourage the artist in someone, write an honest poem.
I have always sung my own song
even when I forget the words or got them wrong
I have always sung my own song.

But now it is different
now it is just me
the things I discovered I could do
have been done.

I'm not the kind of man
who wants to go on doing
what he did before
or even go back and do
what I missed out on before.

We are meant to discover
meet new things
make new connections.

I have rebelled against my family
only to come back and find them
I have got married, divorced
and remained friends

I have brought women joy
I have written songs, formed bands
been cheered to the rafters
I have played to empty rooms
I have nursed a pregnant wife
cradled babies
nursed post-natal and bi-polar
too often to count
I have gained two grandsons
and lost a granddaughter
I have been loved
and hated
despised and respected
admired and detested
acknowledged and neglected
I have lived a life.
So, what's next?

When I look back over my shoulder
I can see the footprints of where I have been.

2. Hair.

When the minister talked about "crowning glory"
I knew what he meant.
My mother wore her hair short in a wartime style
all her life.
It got shorter over the years
as she withdrew
but it was crowning.
My father went bald young
so when my hair darkened and thickened and waved
I imagined that I knew whose son I was.

When a man is in his sixties he becomes invisible
except in his memories.
I have a vague recollection of gliding into a room
thick, dark, wavy, shoulder length hair
levitating me
like the pull of a black halo
a cloud of power
radiance, gravity,
lightening somewhere
glory.

Maybe it felt like that once
maybe it didn't
you can't trust memories
too easy to make them up
then where are you?

Now my hair is greying
but still dark from a distance
my forehead is higher
but there is still plenty on top.
I don't really know what to do with it now
when I was young
freaks grew their hair
straights cut it short
it wouldn't mean the same today
I don't know what it would mean.

But when I touch it, it means something.
When I write the elbow of my left arm rests on the desk
and my fingers comb, stroke, pull at my hair
and it feels like my soul thinking,
like a fish through the reeds
emanation
illumination
crowning.

3. Eyes.

I always thought I looked quite gentle
but I can only ever see them in the mirror
so you will have to draw your own conclusion.

Some people find them fierce and it is true
they can hold you, pin you to the wall,
but not hurt you, not pin you like a butterfly
but hold you in place long enough for you to notice me
and for me to notice you
and to allow the gentleness to settle on you.

Like rain on a forest
like moonlight on a lake
like sun on a beach
and who wouldn't want that?
They seem to ask
you'd be surprised how many didn't.

Those eyes expect something from you
some think they are spoiling for a fight
I think its engagement
like fire is engaged
yes you might be consumed
but I want you to bring your eyes
and I want you to be engaged

There is fear
there is risk
there is vulnerability
a city without gates.

4. The Face Of The Devil.

Swollen, bloated, porcine
fat cheeks, little ears
a sack filled with water
he has a face like an over-stuffed sofa
and there is an invitation for you to sit on it

It is the face of someone who has tasted every poison
licked every honeycomb, nibbled every lotus

Shoulders rounded forward
as if ready to hug
ready to embrace
ready to give comfort
or to embrace a new discovery
a new poison
ready to absorb
this is the Devil in the guise of a bear
a bear in the guise of the Devil
you might find him in the Vatican
or the Kremlin
connecting him with him,
a word in the right place.

5. Seven.

I remember me
I was thirty six
I wasn't very happy
but then looking back
I've never been very happy
but I had the vitality of youth
]to see me through.

Slim, enthusiastic
bouncy, erect, potent,
an electric guitar
tunes that an audience
could sing along with
and lyrics to cast a spell
over the girls.

And then the thing
that I was doing went away
I didn't know
what human life is for
but the thing that
I was doing was
wife and family
and it went away.

I saw the damage
it was doing to my kids
and so I tried to help
single dad for a long time
job in town

I didn't notice
what it was doing
to me.

I buried it
I ate my sadness
I drank my anger
I swallowed my despair
I silenced it all
I had a job to do
don't worry about me

suppressed
depressed
distressed
broken
fat
impotent
sad.

Time for me
to turn and face me
time for me

to go back
and rescue me
like I tried with others
now I'll try with me.

6. Embrace The Shadow.

When the sun strikes me from a certain angle
I cast four shadows
and one of them has a tail.

One can purr and bite
rub its head against your legs
and curl up on your lap
and eat all there is to eat

One is on a white horse
with a sword and shield
dripping dragon's blood
and with blazing eyes for the damsel

then a cloud moves
and the shadows scatter
like bats bursting
on the moonlight

One shadow cannot be reached
it hides in the light
hypnotised and paralysed
safe in inertia

Another shadow holds the pen
advances with his eyes closed
padding the walls with his soul

singing his heart with his soul
he picks up his lyre
and speaks truths
outside of any definition
they are not true, they are not lies
they are magic light multiplying
and when the sun hits them
at a certain angle
they are shadows.

7. The Forest.

I make my own footprint
and no footprint is strange to me

You can see me
You can walk towards me
or walk away

You can see me

This is my path
walk with me a while.

And in the end
I see a lot of wonderful people
in this world
but there is no one I would rather be
than me.

Some of the branches
reach higher than any others
clear of the rest of the forest
and leaves still bud every year
other branches are broken
barely hanging on
some still support a tree house
for adventure, escape and seeing further.
Some give perch to birds

listening to their song
and putting that song in next season's leaves.
This tree occupies its own space
its roots are deep
and I know they work
they can feed me
and anyone who comes to climb these branches

I have known thunder
I have known storm
I have withstood hurricanes
I have known sunshine
I have known shepherds
passing through
I have known lumberjacks
and pesticides
but my roots are deep
and I will stand
I am tree
I am forest

I have heard the song of the birds
I have heard the door-mouse sing
I have heard the fox and her cubs
I have heard the wolf
and the mountain
I have heard the moon
and the clouds
I have heard the eagle
and the raven

the magpie, the finch
and the sparrow
I have heard man, woman and child
ringing through the world
like the blood in my veins
like the sound of the rain
and in the sound of the rain
you will hear my name

I am all these things
I am in the lightening
I am in the snow
I am in the thunder
I am in the river's ceaseless flow
I am in the roar of the bear
I am in the roar of the tiger
I am in the roar and the wingbeat of the dragon
guarding the gates of Hell
and when all of these things have passed
and silence falls
like ash after the fire
like moonlight on the lake
like my finger on your skin
when silence falls
I will still be here
and in that silence
and in that moonlight
and in that skin
I will turn birdsong into leaves.

Notes.

Find out more about Jon on the link -
www.jonbickley.com

Printed in Great Britain
by Amazon